Stay Safe!

Your Own Safety

Sue Barraclough

Heinemann Library
Chicago, Illinois

© 2008 Heinemann Library
a division of Reed Elsevier Inc.
Chicago, Illinois

Customer Service 888-454-2279
Visit our website at www.heinemannraintree.com

Illustrated by Paula Knight
Designed by Joanna Hinton-Malivoire
Picture research by Erica Martin
Printed and bound in China by South China Printing Co. Ltd.
12 11 10 09 08
10 9 8 7 6 5 4 3 2 1

ISBN 10-digit: 1-4034-9858-X (hc) 1-4034-9865-2 (pb)

The Library of Congress has cataloged the first edition of this book as follows:
Barraclough, Sue.
  Your own safety / Sue Barraclough.
     p. cm. -- (Stay safe)
  Includes bibliographical references and index.
  ISBN-13: 978-1-4034-9858-8 (hc)
  ISBN-13: 978-1-4034-9865-6 (pb)
  1. Safety education--Juvenile literature. 2. Children and strangers--Juvenile literature. 3. Children--Crimes against--Prevention--Juvenile literature. I. Title.
  HQ770.7.B37 2008
  613.6083'4--dc22
                              2007016491

Every effort has been made to contact copyright holders of any material reproduced in this book. Any omissions will be rectified in subsequent printings if notice is given to the publishers.

The paper used to print this books comes from sustainable resources.

Contents

You are special.
You need to stay safe.

Do you know how to stay safe?

Never stay alone with a stranger.

Always have a grown-up nearby.

Never do something that makes you feel unsafe.

Always trust your feelings.

Never go anywhere with a stranger.

Always know who is picking you up.

Never do what a stranger asks.

Always say, "No."

Never help a stranger.

14

Always tell them to ask a grown-up.

Never take presents from a stranger.

Always say, "No, thank you."

Never stay where you feel it is not safe.

Always ask a trusted grown-up for help.

Always know your address.

Always know your phone number.

Always remember these safety rules.

Safety Rules

- Never go anywhere on your own.
- Know who is picking you up from school.
- Say, "No" to a stranger.
- Tell strangers to ask a grown-up for help.
- If a stranger gives you a present, say, "No, thank you."
- Go to a trusted grown-up for help.
- Know your address and phone number.
- Trust your feelings.

Picture Glossary

 **feeling** something that you feel inside. You can feel safe or scared.

 **stranger** person you do not know

 **trusted grown-up** someone who can help you. A police officer or teacher can help you.

Index

Note for Parents and Teachers

Books in this series teach children basic safety tips for common situations they may face. Ask children who helps keep them safe (parents, friends, teachers, police). Talk about how these people help, such as by taking them to school, picking them up from school, taking care of them at home, when shopping, or helping them if they are lost. Ask children to identify the trusted adults in their lives.

The text has been chosen with the advice of a literacy expert to ensure beginning readers success when reading independently or with moderate support.

You can support children's nonfiction literacy skills by helping students use the table of contents, picture glossary, and index.